Marnie Prange

DANGEROUS NEIGHBORHOODS

Cleveland State University Poetry Center

This volume is the winning selection in the Montana Arts Council's 1993 First Book Award Competition. It is published in cooperation with the Montana Arts Council by the Cleveland State University Poetry Center. All rights are reserved to the author. Funding for this project was received, in part, from the National Endowment for the Arts.

ISBN 1-880834-70-3

Library of Congress Catalog Card Number: 93-71913

ACKNOWLEDGMENTS

My thanks to the editors of the following publications
in which these poems first appeared.

Black Warrior Review: "Suicide at the 'L' Motel, Flagstaff, AZ"

Cardinal (An Anthology of North Carolina Writers): "Key West, 1953"

CutBank: "Imprimatur," "The Woman Asleep in Our Bed," "With What
Is Left"

*Elvis in Oz: New Poems and Stories from the Hollins Creative Writing Pro-
gram*: "A Fear of High Places"

Intro 12: "Listening to the Blind"

The Louisville Review: "Insomnia," "Cut," "The Burning Bush," "One
on Whom Nothing Is Lost," "Mother Anger," and "Living Alone"

The Missouri Review: "I Want Back In"

The New Virginia Review: "The Tutorial"

Poetry Miscellany: "Wild Apples"

Poetry Northwest: "Key West, 1953," and "No One Was Out: A Letter"

"Failure" and "Suicide at the 'L' Motel, Flagstaff, AZ" won first prize in
the National Poetry Competition of the Hackney Literary Awards. My
thanks to the award sponsors.

Special gratitude to Vicky Anderson-Schiff and to my friends in the
Rattlesnake Ladies' Salon.

CONTENTS

for Greg

Dangerous Neighborhoods

i.

ONE ON WHOM NOTHING IS LOST

The liquor store on the corner
bears the name Friendly Spirits,
a small delight for one
who delights in the literal.
I was in there yesterday, making
my usual purchase. The guy
in front of me was in trouble.
He wanted to return a pack of Salems
bought the day before, wanted
his money back. The package
looked okay, a little
squashed around the edges, but not
so you'd notice. The clerk
shook his head, nope, no way.
When I gave him a five
for a six pack and paper, I wanted
the hand held out for change
to be somebody else's. I stayed
there studying what I didn't need
until the guy and his Salems
were gone. A few days ago
some men had followed me home.
Hey girl, hey girl, they said,
hey, girl on the sidewalk. I knew
who they were talking to, but I looked
down the street and in the yards
for another girl. I wanted
to turn around and say
stop this, and tell them
how I knew I was going to heaven.
A man in front of a Quik Stop
told me so once and meant it
when I gave him a beer and my change.
The last wino I talked to didn't want
any money. Seated on the library steps,

he wanted to know, he said,
if I thought my mouth big enough
to go around his dick. Simply
returning my books, I couldn't keep
from considering his question.
I found the call numbers for geometry,
for sex education, for the bible
and the seven deadly sins. Hours later
the wino was gone, but someone
was chirping at me. I've heard two men
lounging behind cupped palms turn
an entire mall into an aviary that way.
Then it was only the black-capped sparrow
lounging in a tree. One more bottled spirit
making his music from the inside out.

LIVING ALONE

The female rufous hummingbird
is a pig. After she drinks
she hovers for hours, flashing
her white tail bars:
this is mine, this is mine.
All day I hover near the window
watching her. The males come
like comets out of the sky and she
chases them away. I find myself
at the refrigerator, eating this
and then that in her interludes.
I grow fat. A braver person
would remove the feeder. A violent
person would fill it with honey
water and induce the mold
that rots the hummingbird's beak.
I am neither. I have taken
to squirting honey from the bear
into my tea. At first just
a drop, but now his whole head.
I believe my teeth have yellowed,
there is crust around my lips.
This is a predictable poem
and you know what's going to happen.
All day I sing "If my friends could
see me now." My friends,
they're so easy to chase away.

HER FATHER'S DAUGHTER

When my father takes me aside to tell me
about the four sacks of silver he buried
to save his children the future, I think
he's kidding. I want to tell him
I can't bank on the collapse, or to make up
some dumb metaphor—how each two-bit
coin asleep in its sack is like a child
I must soon decide on. Yet when he shows me
the four spindly bushes, I doubt mine will last
the week and take this as a sign my sack
is largest—a huge heart bound by roots.
My father talks of deficits, the waste of investment,
paper money as insubstantial as birds, and I think
of another hole he dug—the bombshelter
he built in the '60's, with a badminton court on top.
Above me, my sisters and brother knocked the birdie
back and forth while I sulked among the tin cans,
the underground daughter waiting for the end.
Now when my father gets down on his knees
to bank the plants against the winter, I kneel
to help him. How like his hands my hands look
as we gather in stray wisps of pinestraw, as we
pat the beds, shape the fragrant nests.

SUICIDE AT THE "L" MOTEL, FLAGSTAFF, AZ

They've blown up our room and left a note:
bad luck and car trouble wore us down.
We sort through the evening paper, through
the wreckage of our own first night in town.
Hard to believe this was us six months ago,
seventeen hours into a head wind, mountain
like a magnet pulling us in, then ten
miles of juke joint and tourist trap.
The first "dying Indian" we saw looked dead.
Hard to believe I wept hard tears, afraid
of the pines. I don't remember smoking.
I don't remember an alias—we didn't need
to think one up. Those also-knowns took
the last name "Promise," Lisa and Lloyd.
Every hotel bragged a view, the "L" overlooked
the Purina Plant, belching the last breaths
of horses that made the dead west great.
All night pickups ground gears
at our window. I don't remember turning
on the gas against the August chill.
Those two children, those masters of irony,
chose Christmas Eve. Like saints
on their knees in front of the pilot,
they blew their last hope out. Dead
two days later, then the charges dropped.
Victims of circumstance, the paper reads.
Victims of our own small hope, the promise
of a new town, in the morning we chose
black coffee from the Jack-in-the-Box
around the corner, strong cigarettes
from the liquor store open at dawn,
and the idea of horses rising in the desert
from the restless breath of sleep.

A FEAR OF HIGH PLACES

for Dara Wier

Imagine the Japanese tourist
at Grand Canyon, just arrived.
Exuberant, happy to be here,
his gesture to the woman
seated in his car
is to leap onto the low wall
that marks the parking lot's perimeter.

Imagine his surprise
when he finds himself
on the canyon rim, nothing
but air rising to meet him.
He wavers an awful instant
on the edge. His arms
outstretched, he looks like
some madcap diver
readying for flight.

Who knows
what he's thinking.
But when he regains
his balance, he steps down
from the wall on legs
that are new and strange.
He turns to the woman
still seated in the car.
Fumbling with her seatbelt,
her handbag, a map
that won't fold, she's missed
one of the important moments
of his life.

A middle-age couple
stands a few yards away.
Out of their element, the safe
green of the east, they step
tentatively toward what
they recognize as the abyss.
They lock hands and look down
seeing for the first time
what they had been up against.

The young man they had caught
with their breath, held
in their lungs, kept
from falling until the canyon
gave up, smiles at them.
This is our honeymoon, he says,
as if in apology.
The three of them look
toward his wife, who is just now
getting out of the car,
and the couple smiles back at him,
softening his fear, calling it
their own.

LISTENING TO THE BLIND

Their names for things
are names we've never heard of,
and they repeat them
slowly, until our ears open wide
and we know the depth of water
under ice, the slow pull
of rain as it effaces
the contours of our bodies.

I heard a man
tell a woman, your body
is an aspen when I want it
to be an aspen. She grew leaves
that dipped silver in the wind.

The blind talk in tongues
of places they've never been.
I want to tell them how
it is: rain falling
on the streets becomes a mirror
I see into, my face,
tears falling from others' eyes.

AT THE ST. IGNATIUS MISSION, MONTANA

No wonder the Indians gave up
their Gods. The plump blond faces
of angels floating on the walls
look like the cornfed faces
of students I taught in Missouri
("Misery" I called it then). Surely
it was the image of nutrition
that saved the Salish souls
and not these cold cathedrals.
The Indians had cathedrals
of their own: out the window
the mountains rise straight
from the valley floor, huge icebergs
just floated up. Against the wall,
in back, two paintings: on the left,
Mary as squaw with Jesus as papoose.
On the right, Our Lord as Salish warrior,
complete with bonnet and ermine tassels,
His right hand raised in effeminate
benediction. Over the dark pews
He looks, past the sailing cherubs,
the seraphim, the saints, ignoring
the Stations of the Cross, his gaze
implacable, bereft. Funny
how they painted the Sacred Heart.
He wears it on the buckskin hide
of his shirt, a valentine directly above
the abdomen. It looks to be looped
with barbwire, or the inept stitches
of a surgical quack. Above it
burns the Cross. And just gingerly
raised to touch it, the tapered fingers
of His left hand. As if the smallest
pressure might unseal the wound, might
start it bleeding all over again.

KEY WEST, 1953

for my mother

A woman skin dives
in the clear water of the Gulf.
She is not afraid
as she waves to her husband
who is moving away from her,
just now moving
out of reach. She waves
and the curious fish
curve away from her fingers.
Now her surprised hands
choreograph an imitation
of water: the fish move
where she wants them to move.
Soon a whole sea of fish
and she forgets the sea
she came for. She thinks
of Venice and the pigeons
circling an old man's head, diving
for pellets of bread balanced
on a hat rim; or, of something
more precise. She is beyond thought.
How could it be otherwise?
All elements are fish, her body
the question they answer.
She sways and the fish sway
with her. Wrapped in a movement
of silver, she becomes the fish
the silver curtain moves
on its current. She might
be taken out to sea,
to the sargasso weeds
at its center, wear a wreath
of mourning to her evening bed,

dress herself in coral.
Or, she might stay here forever.
Become translucent as fish,
sea-softened back
into an earlier, easier shape.
The danger escapes her
until out of the magic of fish
comes her husband. He takes her hand
and she kicks her legs, following.
Safe from the secret underwater
touching, her body turns
back into itself. Here
are her ankles, her impossible
thighs. She will not undress again
in this hall of mirrors,
before these underwater eyes.

TRYING TO GET HOME

It isn't easy.

There's always the cop
putting me under arrest
for parking my car
the wrong way on the wrong
side of the street.

I call him boss traffic.

He invites me up
to his room. I'd like
to go, but the elevator
is on the fritz.
Down is all it's doing.

He slips around the corner,
comes back dressed
as the repairman
I've always dreaded.

So I say, "No, thank you,"
and turn, and leave,

and lose my way.
Wind up downtown
where no one ever
is supposed to be.

A man in a window
washing dishes
tells me, go this way,
and then this.
He throws me his dishrag.
Like a flag, I carry it
in front of me.

I call him the soldier.

I take his directions
but I don't follow them.
It's a dangerous neighborhood
I choose, darkness
in every home.

When the repairman steps
out from behind his van,
any fool can see
he isn't here for business.

I cross my fingers
and hope he's the cop
I can con. I say,
"Let's go try that elevator."

He buys it.
I call him the cashier.

I take his change,
and I take my clothes
to the washeteria.
Turn my back,
and the only guy
in the place

takes out his pen
and prints his phone number
across the butt
of my best panties.
I wink at him.

I call him Jimmy.
It's written on his shirt.

When I find my way home
he'll already be there,
behind the refrigerator
making it work.

ii.

CHILDHOOD

Weekend mornings we woke at dawn,
watched "Shock Theater," sipped the dregs
of martinis, dragged butts. Our parents
slept late, hungover from the previous
nights' parties. Aliens, ghosts, homicidal
maniacs—nothing unsettled the headache quiet.
Afternoons sleep-walked into evening,
a background hum of football, our parents' touches
small ignitions that moved them through the day.
A paragon of resolve, weekdays our mother
rose first to ready us for school.
But the eggs she placed in front of us were cold,
the toast burned, the table set for unhappiness:
our father would not get out of bed to go to work.
Emissaries from the foreign country of our fear,
one by one we'd tiptoe into the spermy halflight
of their room. *Dad-dy*, we'd whine. And beg him
to get up before Mommy came. He'd grunt, roll over,
fall back asleep until Mommy did come
—a fury in black ponytail and red lipstick,
tearing back the covers, ripping the pillow
from his head. Under the banner of housework
she'd start in on the rugs. We'd flee for the bus,
while behind us the roar of the vacuum
roused the living dead.

I WANT BACK IN

Let me in the door, he yells,
his small fists pounding,
let me in the door.

We call him half of that,
our neighbor across the street.
Let Me In.

If anyone at his house is ever home,
I can't tell. Nor can he.
I know how he feels.

Even riding his Big Wheel
up and down the sidewalk, he's angry.
I'd like to tell him

it's anger that shuts him out.
Be nice, I'd say. He wouldn't listen.
Five years old is enough

to know how far niceness goes.
He takes it out on his dog.
Bewildered as he,

the dog won't cower either.
It keeps fetching the same bad stick.
And each afternoon,

when the schoolbus spits him out,
the dog is the only one waiting,
tail tucked and wagging.

MOTHER ANGER

Now I am angry all morning
stacking up injustices
with each cruddy plate.
Egg yolk is enough
to sicken, the slimy
umbilical cords
I pushed to the side
slop in the drain.
Run the hot water over my hands
till they scald pure
as boiled milk.
Against his shirt I'm wearing
my nipples stiffen and burn.
What's wrong now, nobody asks me.
Write a letter.
Send it to your mother.

CUT

I am slicing strawberries,
my knife poised

over the next one, plump
between thumb and forefinger.

There is a slight pull.
I can't tell,

is knife after thumb,
or thumb, knife?

I can hardly resist it.
The juice of berries

already cut is my blood
coming out of me

and falling. The knife
is a grin on the floor.

Driving to the hospital,
around the highway curve

a woman caught in my headlights
is running toward me.

Her clothes are off and her arms.
Someone has taken her arms.

She opens her mouth to call,
and someone has taken her tongue.

If I put her in my car,
how can I talk to her?

Can I offer her a cigarette,
explaining, "The hospital,

I don't know where it is."
Because I have, of course,

forgotten. But what if I remember
the number? Do I make that call?

Then proceed on my way
as though nothing has happened

until I drive head-on into
the ambulance coming to help her,

and it's me they help instead.
They lift me on their table.

The surgeons are already ready
to go for the throat.

Is their nothing they can give me
to make me go under?

THE TUTORIAL

In this country, her imagination is full
of Venezuela and what she must translate.
Aura is in love, telling me I look
just like her best friend. The first time
she saw me, she almost cried.
She reads to me and her voice belongs
to the rain in the distance. Beyond us,
I am a woman walking beside a field
of men who dig with sticks
for the root of the cassava. That woman
stops and gives her hands to a man
the color of the earth he turns.
She is tall and fair and when she points
to the mountains that surround
the Gran Sabaña, her arm is a compass
needle pointing north. But for his eyes,
which see only the mountains, the man
could be her lover. He could be the one
whose hands warm her thighs in the cool nights,
whose hands implore her silence.
When she turns to leave him, he must know
something of the mountains in her,
must hear the Churun roar in her footsteps.
Aura's voice. Her foreign tongue.
It is time of enjoy by all people.
Indians light candles and dance to drums
imagined in distant Caracas. Beyond them
the shrouded mountains, the forest wet and thick.
At its edge the woman burns like a wick.
From her mouth come words no longer foreign.
Aura cannot answer why the woman
is there, what syllables spill from her tongue.

HER DREAM OF CLAY PIGEONS

In her dream, in the same glare
she shaded earlier from her eyes, she sees

the black and yellow flashes in the sun
as finches. Now she would

save souls from their bodies, falling
in mid-air, shot free

in flight from the living. She presses
the gun to her cheek, the barrel

swaying like a carried ladder,
like one she would extend

from her own falling body
to climb free. In the morning,

in her bruised shoulder,
she finds the colors that are hers.

WITH WHAT IS LEFT

i.

Let's bury them face down, the thieves
and cheaters among us. Those who
have taken our husbands and wives,
who have spoken ill of us, and not
paid their debts. Imagine them
with bedsores, trying to turn.
This much we know for certain.
If we don't help them they will stay
like that forever. I like to think
of them forever staring back
into the empty socket of their skulls,
thinking the porcelain shine
they see is the moon. It is the rim
of what's left when what's left is nothing.

ii.

The ones who died sick with sickness
still inside, let's give a second chance.
Say we bury them with water and food.
If resourceful, they can heal themselves
and go whole into the next life.
Isn't the next life the one we want
to be healthy in? Let's pray now
for no temptation in the hereafter.
Grind our cigarettes into the ground,
let the whole earth's rivers run gold
with our whiskey. We won't care.
We have forsaken all that kills us.
We are dead and buried
with our water and our good wheat bread.

iii.

Those of us who were saints in this life,
or wanted to be, let's cover their faces
with dishes from the ancient tribes.
Let's make a hole in each dish, let's make
them no good for water. Where saints go
they don't need water. They don't need
the invisible, the see-through,
what they've already got. It's what
they've always wanted. Give me the bowl
I like best, the one with two hands
at its center, spreading apart earth's lips.
Let those hands be mine. I want out
while the getting out is good.

iv.

Isn't each one of us a saint and sick
to death of it? The one same cheater
guarding his necessary lie? Ignore us.
Bury us any way you choose.
It doesn't matter. We've given up the game.
We're each of us already dead and buried
in the grave we dug our whole lives long.
We call it the heart—that empty place
we carry inside, the one we've tailor made
until it is the fit we try on for size.
We slip in easy. We learn to live there,
unafraid of any thief but ourselves,
who will end by leaving us nothing.
We slip in easy. We learn to live there.

iii.

THE WOMAN ASLEEP IN OUR BED

is not mine, which must mean
it was you who placed her there.
Surely this is not my imagination.
See how she wakes and smiles up
at us so warmly, trying to please,
as we stand at the foot of our bed.
Isn't she pleasant, and why
won't she speak? Notice there is room
for three of us, if I don't mind
sleeping close to the wall
and we each agree neither
to toss nor turn, but to guard
our positions carefully
until sleep has taken us all.
Have you warned her
how I call out in my dreams
and what I say is so funny,
though often distracting?
Isn't it time we all went to bed?
Notice how beautiful her hair
in this yellow light, or
perhaps you planned it so
to entrance me. Of course you did.
You think of everything.
But how long is she staying,
and what is her name?
And does this mean she is mine,
as well as yours?

THE PROFESSORS AT THE FAIR

Connie Barnett is selling
at auction her champion steer.
Connie is eleven we are told,
and we see for ourselves
she is blond and shy.
Too close to the microphone
when she speaks, she whispers
she wants to by a Simmental heifer
with the proceeds from the steer
we now suspect is unworthy.
After the champion goats, the turkeys
and lambs, we're sick of the kids
who want to go to college
and all for Connie. We applaud wildly
as she turns her steer towards us,
then away, displaying his dubious
charms. We know nothing of cattle
but we admire his straightness
of leg, his large bovine eyes.
That's it, Connie, we yell.
Stay home on the farm!
Our enthusiasm astounds us.
We're the ones who drifted in
from the midway, from the corn dogs
and elephant ears, the rides
we let swallow our stomachs,
the games we fed dimes.
The hucksters we left behind us
with their promises of miracles.
The ones we bought we carry
like secrets in brown paper bags:
gadgets to turn radishes into roses,
slippers lined with water
to keep our weight off our feet.
Each one of us just looking

for a place to sit down.
The men who came here to bid
catch on. Their raises
are outrageous. We applaud
our approval. Our Connie approves.
She blushes at just the right price.
We are in love.
We want to live with Connie
down on her farm, roll
in her blue ribbon hay, drink
that milk and honey.
The steer is finally sold
and we can't contain our happiness.
Bring on the chickens!
Bring on the hogs!
A little less luxury,
please!

TRIPPING THE LIGHT FANTASTIC

The multi-faceted globe spins
above the dance floor and the light
it throws *is* fantastic, as my grandparents
go round and round, grandpa spinning grandma,
holding her in his arms—when holding anyone
was so difficult for him to do.
I remember paint and pinecones. Everything
at his house he spray-painted silver
or forest green (everything he could)—
wooden stools, garbage cans, the handles
of rakes and shovels. At Christmas
we went there to decorate the pinecones
he had collected, spraying them silver
or forest green, then a red dust of glitter.
We were little kids then and he was like
a new kindergarten teacher, generous,
solicitous, handing out eight-ounce Cokes
and miniature candy bars. We played "Moose"
together, guess the ornament, sang rounds
of "Oh, Christmas Tree" in German,
his native tongue. I had to grow up
and go away to recognize his distance:
my grandfather never touched me.
Home from college, then college teaching,
each Christmas morning I greeted my grandparents
at the top of my parent's stairs. Grandma,
a quick kiss and long hug, grandpa,
a handshake. I mistook it for coldness,
some lack of caring. Years later,
I understood his lesson—his distance
a preparation for the dialogue of gestures
that would be my heritage with men.
Read the signs, he taught me,
no matter how small and inscrutable.

The sign I remember best was like a billboard:
the Christmas I played my new Tina Turner tape
and my grandfather rose, stiff
and stick-limbed from the depths
of his armchair to ask me to dance.
Round and round he waltzed me while Tina sang
What's love got to do, got to do with it?
Past the Christmas tree we whirled,
with its blowing tinsel, around
the startled dogs with their holiday rawhide,
to end, finally, in front of the family.
Gathered around the morning's presents,
they looked up to see us there, amazed,
as we saw ourselves, reflected in their eyes.
I leaned against the strength I trusted
in my grandfather's arm and he bent me back
against the suppleness he trusted in my spine—
low, lower still, until my hair swept the floor
and I threw back my arm for balance.

WILD APPLES

Up through the laurel
and loblolly pine we followed
my parents, our goal
the mountaintop and the highland cattle
we'd been told we'd find foraging
in thickets of rhododendron.
Ginseng, we'd heard, was grown there,
that medicinal herb the branch
we followed was named for.
The path was steep. We stopped
often for my father to show us
the sights. A flat rock perfect
for resting. A fence post
that had taken root. Cut from green wood
decades ago, it encased the wire
tacked into it. We learned
the names of plants, the history
of the shelves of rock
that breached the mountainside.
You had just met my parents
and you were interested in everything.
You could not see
how my mother fell behind,
how my father lingered in explanation.
I heard my own heart beat
for the hearts of my parents.
When the trail opened into the valley
of a dead farm, we found
a wild apple tree, rooted
in a clear spring. We pulled down
the swollen apples, swore
we could taste the water they grew from.
Further up we found the farmhouse
and more trees, apples like hard plums,
and heart-shaped apples

the color of clotted blood. My father
tied the arms of his jacket
and we loaded the sack he had made.
In the vinegar air we talked
of pies and popovers, brown betty
and the cider we might press
in our separate kitchens. The sack
was heavy. When you slung it over
your shoulder and offered to carry
it back down, we turned to each other
agreeing, wild apples were enough.

INSOMNIA

Outside, the moon rivals
the dogs. Inside,
it is quiet.
The moon, suspended
in the mirror of our window,
watches itself rise.
This is only my idea.
You are asleep, your breath
beside me taken and held.
What are your dreams
that I might enter them
and be held?

The traffic washes down
Sixth Street, calling me
to the window
that watches me rise.
I am translucent,
electric in my loneliness,
in my white night gown.
All the busy motorists
pass me by. If I could
somehow join them,
go with them to their
curious destinations.
And what would they see

if they looked toward
my window? Their headlights
in the glass, more moons
catching nothing.
If I stood at the window
and turned from it,
I would see your clothes,
heaped on the floor, sleeping

even as they slid off
of you—you, a curve
under the covers
gesturing *here, come to bed.*

I want to enter you
and be held.
Lie my full length down
in the dark of your body.
I know what I'm asking.
I want what you have.

FAILURE

You and my father were in
his flat-bottom boat, behind
a stand of weeds in the middle
of a large slough. I was on the bank,
low in the grass, watching.
Earlier my father had told me
how my face frightened the ducks,
a bright moon in the weeds
staring up at them. Now I kept my face
hidden. When ducks flew over, my father
winged one, and it flew over me, low,
then over the rise of a ploughed field.
I saw it go down and crossed the field
after it, found the pothole
it had found, full of bright weeds
I couldn't name. And I found the duck,
a mallard, flattened in the grass,
not a mark on it. When it waddled
away from me, dragging a wing, I knew
I would have to kill it. I could
kill it, I had seen it done before.
I took it by the neck and swung it
sharply in a circle as I had seen my father
swing ducks that weren't quite dead.
But the duck didn't die and I flung it
against the ground, and again
when it didn't die, I wrung its neck,
held it by the head and cracked
its body like a whip. And again.
All around me the prairie held its breath.
In the silence of that live duck,
that broken contract, I understood
that I was helpless. I cradled the duck
in my arms and carried it back to you
across the field, called to my father

who has the magic of death. When you finally
rowed in to me at dusk, the duck lay dead
at my side. My father, you told me,
as you admired its size, was worried.
He wanted me to like hunting, to like
the great outdoors. I thought what a waste
that the duck I tried to kill
and then wanted to save was dead
and so was so much more.
You let my father let you fail me.

IMPRIMATUR

One winter I lay down in front
of my lover in the snow and said the words
precision and *beauty*. And though
it was dark and I could not see his face,
which I knew to be precise and beautiful,
I saw the nodding pines behind him nod
their affirmation. So I swept my arms slowly
up against the snow and slowly back
against my sides to rest, stood up then
and admired with my amazed lover the angel
pressed by my body in the snow.
Now when I lie down with my lover
the angels my body keeps lie down with us,
and when I take his hands in mine and spread
our arms wide like wings extended
we press an angel into our bed
readying for flight.

NO ONE WAS OUT: A LETTER

No one was out this afternoon
when I walked the beach
in front of our cottage, but you
had been out before. I chose
your footprints and imitated
the limp I found in your gait,
the way the ball of your left foot
pushes deep in the sand.
I wanted to go on like that forever,
following a man I could never
catch up with. I went on
until the island came to a point
and the shorebirds gave up
their fear. They saw
that I was nothing, the afterimage
of the man who had come before.

When I came home to tell you
this story, I was told to hush.
A heron was wading the lagoon
at the back of our cottage,
fishing the dim light our porch
cast on the water. You caught him
in your fieldglasses and gave them
to me to look. The blue heron
I saw as white ringed by darkness,
an inverted silhouette stalking
its prey. Its legs that had been
sticks in daylight
moved with unspeakable precision,
as if it were walking on glass.
I could not look away.

After whiskey and talk we went
to bed. We heard only the sound
of the ocean, rocking us

as we rocked in love. I was glad
to think of our bed at home
and the radio you thought
we'd forgotten, keeping its own
dull time. I was sorry
when I woke you in the night,
when I sat up stunned and asked
Who are you? In the morning,
you told me I had fallen quickly
back to sleep. I told you
I was simply bewildered by the beach,
which was half of the truth.

THE BURNING BUSH

The neighbors are out of their houses
and their faces are as real as mine.
I want to see them glowing
from the flame's heat, but it's afternoon
and the fire is out, the firemen gone.
They did their duty across the street,
putting out the flame any one
of our garden hoses could have drowned.
We stand around, shy and tentative,
unwilling to go home. I watch
what's left of the bush take shape.
Its growing had not been easy.
I see this in the trunk, how it went
one way and then another, frantic
in its choice of direction
until its growing twisted and curled.
Secretly I applaud whoever burned
the bush. I suspect the neighbors.
I'd like us to lock hands and circle
the dying tree. Some of us would weep,
some would burst into song.
When daylight failed, I'd give
each neighbor a limb of the bush
to carry like a torch into his home.
We would nurture the bush back into flame.
Our houses would be flares in the night
for anyone to find us.

NOTES

The title "One on Whom Nothing Is Lost" is adapted from a familiar passage in Henry James's "The Art of Fiction."

The penultimate lines of "With What Is Left" are adapted from the closing of Katherine Ann Porter's short story "Theft": "She laid the purse on the table and sat down with a cup of chilled coffee, and thought: I was right not to be afraid of any thief by myself, who will end by leaving me nothing."